START-UP
ENGLISH
BIOGRAPHIES

MARTIN LUTHER KING

John Malam

Evans

Evans Brothers Limited

Published by Evans Brothers Limited
2A Portman Mansions
Chiltern Street
London W1U 6NR

© in this edition Evans Brothers Limited 2009

Printed in China

Editor: Bryony Jones
Designer: Mark Holt

To find out more about the author visit his website: www.johnmalam.co.uk

British Library Cataloguing in Publication Data

Malam, John
    Martin Luther King. – (Start-up English. Biographies)
    1. King, Martin Luther, Jr., 1929-1968 – Juvenile
    literature. 2. African American civil rights workers –
    United States – Biography – Juvenile literature. 3. Civil
    rights workers – United States – Biography – Juvenile
    literature.
    I. Title II. Series
    323.1'196073'092-dc22

ISBN-13: 9780237538729

Picture acknowledgements: **Cover** (main) Hulton Getty Picture Collection, (top left and right) Associated Press/Topham; Title page Karsh of Ottawa/Camera Press Limited; **page 4** Corbis-Bettmann/UPI; **page 5** Corbis/Bettmann; **page 6** Corbis/Bob Krist; **page 7** (top) Corbis/Bettmann, (bottom) Topham Picturepoint; **page 8** Genevieve Naylor Corbis/Bettmann; **page 9** Corbis; **page 10** Associated Press/Topham; **page 11** Karsh of Ottawa/Camera Press Limited; **page 12** Corbis-Bettmann/UPI; **page 13** Associated Press Limited; **page 14** Corbis-Bettmann/UPI; **page 15** INTERFOTO Pressebildagentur/Alamy; **page 16** Hulton Getty Picture Collection; **page 17** Corbis-Bettmann/UPI; **page 18** Corbis-Bettmann/UPI; **page 19** Hulton Getty Picture Collection; **page 20** Associated Press/Topham; **page 21** Associated Press/Topham

VISIT OUR WEBSITE
Evans
www.evansbooks.co.uk

Contents

Who was Martin Luther King?

In some parts of America, less than 50 years ago, black people were treated badly by white people. Black children were not allowed to mix with white children.

► Black people were not allowed to drink from the same fountains as white people.

America black people white people

►One man, Martin Luther King, wanted to make things better for all black people. He wanted them to be equal to white people.

This is his story.

equal

Birth and parents

In January 1929, Martin Luther King was born in Atlanta, a city in the south of America.

► He lived in a large old house with his parents, grandparents, brother and sister, and uncles and aunts.

MARTIN LUTHER KING, JR.
WAS BORN IN THIS HOUSE
JANUARY 15, 1929

► Martin's father was a Christian **minister** at Ebenezer Baptist Church.

◄ He taught Martin that God had made all people equal.

minister

School and university

When Martin went to school, he went to a school for black children. His white friends went to a school for white children. This separation of blacks and whites was called segregation. It upset Martin.

separation   segregation

After school Martin became a minister. When he was 22 he went to Boston University.

◄ Boston is in the north of America. Black people there were treated better than in the south. Martin started to think about how he could help black people in the south.

Marriage and work

While he was at Boston University Martin met Coretta Scott. They fell in love and got married.

◀ They had four children. Here they are with Yolanda, Martin and Dexter. After this picture was taken they had their fourth child, Bernice.

Martin became the minister in a church in
Montgomery, in the south of America. He was
still upset at the way black people were treated.

Montgomery

Rosa Parks' protest

One day, in 1955, a black lady in Montgomery called Rosa Parks sat in the part of a bus that was just for white people. She refused to move, and was arrested.

refused   arrested

The black people in Montgomery were angry. Martin was their leader. He organised a protest, which lasted for a year.

Many people were arrested, including Martin himself.

Finally, a judge said that the bus company was wrong to separate black people from whites.

leader   protest   judge

Segregation and protest

► **Buses were no longer segregated but shops and restaurants were. They had separate** counters **for blacks and whites to sit at.**

Black people protested all over America.

counters

Martin wanted to help the blacks. In 1957 he stopped being a minister and started to travel around America. He spoke at meetings and wrote books.

travel   meetings

A hero in danger

Martin became a hero for black people. He also had many white supporters. Some white people went to his meetings.

hero   supporters

But it was a
dangerous job.
One day someone
exploded a **bomb**
at his house. Luckily
no one was hurt.

◀ Once, a cross
was burnt outside
Martin's house.

dangerous **bomb**

Arrest and release

In 1963 thousands of adults and children took part in a protest in **Birmingham** in the USA.

The police attacked them with water hoses. Martin was arrested and sent to jail, but was soon released.

Birmingham   jail

He organised another march, in Washington. More than 250,000 people joined in. Martin gave a famous speech. He said, 'I have a dream that my four little children will one day live in a nation where they will not be judged by the colour of their skin....'

speech   nation

Nobel Prize and last speech

In 1964 black people were given equal **rights** to white people. Martin was given a special prize called the **Nobel Peace Prize**.

rights   **Nobel Peace Prize**

Martin continued to work for black people's rights. In 1968 he went to Memphis to give a speech. The next day, as he stood on a balcony, he was shot and killed. America was shocked. Ever since, people have continued Martin's struggle for equal rights.

Key words introduced in the text

America	dangerous	meetings	refused	travel
arrested	equal	minister	rights	university
Birmingham	hero	Montgomery	segregation	white people
black people	jail	nation	separation	
bomb	judge	Nobel Peace Prize	speech	
counters	leader	protest	supporters	

Background Information

Slavery

The first black people in North America were brought as slaves from Africa in 1619, and the slave trade increased greatly in the 1680s. In 18th-century North America, especially in the cotton and rice plantations of the southern states, the slave trade flourished. Slavery was abolished in the United States in 1865, after the American Civil War.

Inequality

The abolition of slavery did not mean equality for black people, however. In the southern states, after the American Civil War, measures were introduced to stop black people from voting, and laws passed to enforce segregation. This was known as the Jim Crow era. Jim Crow was a black character in a song-and-dance act performed by American entertainer Thomas Rice.

'I have a dream'

Martin Luther King's most famous speech was spoken in Washington in 1963, when 250,000 people went on a march. He said, 'I have a dream that my four little children will one day live in a nation where they will not be judged by the color of their skin but by the content of their character… I have a dream that one day… little black boys and black girls will be able to join hands with little white boys and white girls and walk together as sisters and brothers.'

Equality?

2008 marked the fortieth anniversary of Martin Luther King's death. While much has been done to improve the situation of many black people, a question mark still hangs over the question of whether full equality has been achieved. But many saw the inauguration of Barack Obama as US President in January 2009 as a great step forward. He is the first ever African-American president.

Parents and Teachers

Topics for discussion

Do the children know about anyone else who became famous for helping others?

Can they think of jobs in the local community where helping people is an important part of the job?

Can they think of examples of inequality or unfairness in their own lives?

How did they feel about it? Was it possible to make a change?

Suggested activities

Find out about other winners of the Nobel Peace Prize.

Ask the children if they have a dream for the future. Can they give a speech or draw a poster about it?

Recommended resources

Books for young children:
The life of Martin Luther King Jr, Emma Lynch, Heinemann 2006
Martin Luther King (Famous People Famous Lives),
V Wilkins, Franklin Watts 2002

Books for older readers:
Martin Luther King (Judge for Yourself), Christine Hatt,
Evans Brothers, 2009
Rosa Parks and her protest for Civil Rights (Dates with History), Philip Steele, Cherrytree Books, 2007

http://www.historylearningsite.co.uk/martin_luther_king.htm
http://nobelprize.org/nobel_prizes/peace/laureates/1964/king-bio.html
http://www.bbc.co.uk/history/historic_figures/king_martin_luther.shtml

Important dates

1929	15 January – Martin Luther King was born in Atlanta, Georgia, USA
1944	Age 15 – he left school and went to Morehouse College, Atlanta
1948	Age 19 – he left Morehouse College, as a Baptist Minister
1951	Age 22 – he began to study at Boston University
1953	Age 24 – he married Coretta Scott and they settled in Montgomery, Alabama
1954	Age 25 – he became a minister at a church in Montgomery, Alabama
1958	Age 29 – he was stabbed
1959	Age 30 – he left his church
1963	Age 34 – he organised protests in Birmingham, Alabama; during a march in Washington, he gave his famous 'I have a dream…' speech
1964	Age 35 – he was awarded the Nobel Peace Prize
1966	Age 37 – he moved to Chicago, Illinois, to help fight poverty among black people
1968	4 April, age 39 – he was shot dead, in Memphis, Tennessee

Index